T0146716

DOGS

AND

UNORDINARY PEOPLE

DONALD L. DRENNAN

authorHOUSE®

AuthorHouse™
1663 Liberty Drive
Bloomington, IN 47403
www.authorhouse.com
Phone: 1 (800) 839-8640

© 2016 Donald L. Drennan. All rights reserved.

*No part of this book may be reproduced, stored in a retrieval system, or
transmitted by any means without the written permission of the author.*

Published by AuthorHouse 10/31/2016

ISBN: 978-1-5246-2780-5 (sc)
ISBN: 978-1-5246-2778-2 (hc)
ISBN: 978-1-5246-2779-9 (e)

Library of Congress Control Number: 2016914430

Print information available on the last page.

*Any people depicted in stock imagery provided by Thinkstock are models,
and such images are being used for illustrative purposes only.
Certain stock imagery © Thinkstock.*

This book is printed on acid-free paper.

*Because of the dynamic nature of the Internet, any web addresses or
links contained in this book may have changed since publication and may
no longer be valid. The views expressed in this work are solely those
of the author and do not necessarily reflect the views of the publisher,
and the publisher hereby disclaims any responsibility for them.*

Contents

Bouvier

Preface

As a child, I devoured all the dog books from the library, and each month eagerly looked forward to receiving my copy of DOG WORLD magazine. I dreamed of owning and showing top winning dogs. As an adult, my small hobby kennel was the answer to my wishes.

When you are successful in any field, you attract people from all walks of life. It is these people and my dogs that this book is about. Their stories are worth telling. They show we all have one thing in common, the love for Mother Nature's most precious gift, the dog.

Don Drennan

My mommy thinks when I grow up
I could be Mr. America.

BEST WISHES!

Ch. Jena

"The starting point for our hike each day in winter"

My Favorite Dog -
Lona.....A Chow Chow

In July, 1958, I organized a three week trip out West with the intention of hiking for a week in Glacier National Park in Montana. It was on the last day of hiking high in the mountains that I met a young couple with a Chow Chow, very content walking along on a six foot lead. He was a beautiful red and the couple was only too eager to tell me of their adventures with their companion. I had lost a Chow Chow a few years earlier and thought it most unusual that I would meet one so far away in the mountains of Glacier National Park. They enjoyed hearing about my Cherry and that half hour meeting made a real impression on me. I felt then and there I needed another dog and that dog had to be another Chow.

Lona was born in a kennel in North Tonawanda on a snowy December day. She was a red and at six weeks I brought her home. My first requirement was to have a dog with no known genetic faults, a healthy animal that could be obedience trained, walk on long hikes and be a first class companion in all ways. Lona fit that description.

My mother lived with me in the lower flat of a home in Kenmore, N.Y., and my sister, Peggy, her husband and two boys lived upstairs. All were excited to have Lona join us. She was well socialized.

At six months, I entered her in an obedience class taught by well known trainer, Howard Trautwein. He notified me that Chows were very independent and not the easiest to train. Lona proved him wrong. Of all the dogs in our beginner class, she was the first to earn her Companion Dog obedience title at three American Kennel Club shows. You had to have three legs under three different judges to qualify, and on her third and final leg, Lona earned a score of 195 out of a perfect 200. I was delighted.

Lona always slept in my bedroom on the floor beside my bed where it was cool. When I was not home she became very protective of this room. When I was a work my mother would call her and she would leave the bedroom to spend long stretches running free in our fenced in backyard. I took her early on mornings for long walks, and again in the evening.

When we trained for her CD the corner drugstore allowed me to put her on the long down or long sit for three minutes while I left the store and stood outside so she could not see me. Strangers walked in and out and still she would not move. She was an A student.

When I wasn't home she didn't want anyone to enter my bedroom. She would bark and growl at the doorway if anyone came near. She would not let my mother or anyone else in. This was her domain and she guarded it against all intruders. She was a real one-man-dog, followed me everywhere in the house. If I went into the bathroom, I knew she would be lying by the door when I opened it. She never let me out of her sight.

3

"Do I look pretty?

At 2 1/2 years, I decided to breed her to a champion male owned by the kennel where I bought her. She whelped three female puppies, was an excellent mother and weaned them with no problems whatsoever. I sold one to a young woman in West Virginia, the second one to an older couple in Ohio. They never had children and Lulu was spoiled rotten. I kept the third - Sabrina.

I continued to train Lona for the Companion Dog Excellent title. It required the dog to retrieve a dumbell, jump over a broadjump, retrieve a dumbell over a high jump, and, of course, to heel off lead around the ring with stop and goes along the way per the judge's commands. She did qualify for one leg with a score in the eighties.

But at this point Zoar Valley was discovered and our attention each week was exploring our new found dream land. It is 300 acres of fields, woods galore ravines, cliffs, trails to follow and wildlife everywhere. It is a Western New York paradise with Cattaraugus Creek flowing through its flatlands with water deep enough you can swim in it.

Lona felt right at home. I would go down weekends with Lee and Bruce and, of course, Lona. When I let her out of the car the first time, I thought she might run off and leave us. That was not her idea. She spent all her time with me - the devoted one-man dog Chow. I would go on walks and she followed right behind never letting me out of her sight.

Bette, Al and family were always in Zoar each weekend and they, too, bought a large tent for camping over night. I bought one large enough for Lee, Bruce, Lona and myself and Friday and Saturday nights it was our shelter from the night darkness.

I remember one time when I was hiking alone with Lona, she was interested in a rabbit hole so I went on alone to see what she would do. A tree with lower branches and ideal for climbing invited me to climb it, which I did. When I reached the upper branches Lona arrived looking for me. She smelled around the tree where I had stood, but did not look upwards. Something was wrong. There was no scent going forward so she turned around and started back from the way we came. I waited awhile, climbed down and headed back behind her. I never caught up to Lona and became very worried. I remembered how fast I moved to get back to the tent to see if she was there. I was scared something might have happened and she got lost along the way. I never felt so relieved when I saw her at our tent. She jumped with joy, wagging her tail a mile a minute and crying when she saw me in her doggy style voice. I never had such a welcome. That was the last time I ever tried that trick.

It was a wonderful feeling to have the opportunity in such a natural wild Zoar setting to enjoy a dog similar to what the settlers must have had many years ago in the same setting. It was getting close to nature with nature' wonderful creation - a dog - and appreciating the beauty and happiness such an outdoor environment brought us.

At the end of each day, we never had a problem falling asleep in our tent. Lona slept by me and was as tired as the rest of us from the day's activities. We brought our own food, Coleman stove, pots and pans, etc. Sometimes it was very chilly in the mornings.

One Saturday the family all got together to plant trees -200 small young ones in the large field where the land had started to erode and wash the soil downward. The New York State Dept. of Environment recommended Scotch Pines for the area and sold us the tees to be planted in rows just so far apart and a specific distance between each seedling. We worked in pairs. I would place my foot on a spade, open up the ground the depth of the spade and Bruce would insert the small seedling and cover it up with his hands. Lee worked with Al and they always were ahead of the rest of us when we discovered they were planting two seedlings in one hole. They denied it. It was a fun filled day to say the least.

One warm Saturday we were all down in the flat lands where Cattaraugus Creek flows through the property and navigates itself along the bottom of the cliffs that are as high as Niagara on one side. The water was deep at this time of the year. We were lazily throwing stones in the water trying to see how far we could make them jump at one time. Suddenly, we could hardly believe it, but a deer was swimming in the middle of the stream with its head bobbing up and down as the animal was swept along in the strong current. And low and behold, Lona saw it too. She wasted no time, ran into the creek and was swept along behind the deer. I stood frozen in fear as I repeatedly called her name. On and on she went, around the bend and out of sight. We were hopeless to do anything but wait. I called her name repeatedly hoping she might be swept ashore and would return to me. We waited and waited. I never stopped calling her name. Thank goodness dogs have fantastic hearing. Out of no where, walking along the shore on the other side was Lona soaking wet, I never felt more relieved in my life. I called her and she swam across to me with no problem whatsoever. We were reunited and what a happy time that was for both of us. She kept shaking the water off like all dogs do when they get wet. I knew with a dry towel waiting at the tent she would dry out fast on that warm day. The adventure was over. After a good meal at night, we went to bed early. Lona had eaten an extra large portion and I don't think she moved all night. It was a day we will always remember.

Through all our many weekends in Zoar, we did manage, as a family, to build a cabin. Our tents were no longer a necessity. This made it possible to spend more time in colder weather in Zoar where the pot-belly wood burning stove heated the cabin for us. It was on one of these chilly days in November that we decided to head home. The McCarthy's and I parked our cars at the Fowler farm approximately one mile from our cabin, and we had walked down to the cabin when we arrived in Zoar on Saturday morning. I believe the possible weather conditions were why we did not drive down over the dirt road to the property. So on that Sunday about four in the afternoon we headed back to Fowlers and our cars.

Lona was always off lead and followed me up the hill. The dirt road boardered Fowler's and the Zoar property. Fowler's property was fenced in for his small herd of cows let out each day to graze. He had about six or seven and when Lona saw them she went under the fence to invesrigate.

It was at this point I couldn't believe my eyes. Like a trained hearding dog, she instinctly started to nip at their backlegs and barking a message for them to start moving. When one started to move fast towards its barn Lona went after another. Some started to kick with their rear legs but Lona dodged them with ease. She had them all moving together at a fast pace, I was shocked and a sight I will never forget.

I kept thinking what will Fowler say when his cattle suddenly appear out of nowhere. Lona ignored my calls. She had a job to do and no hearding dog could have done it better. I followed as fast as I could in the field, but in no way could I move as fast as my animal friends.

We were almost to the barn when Fowler appeared walking toward us. I started to apologize and told him I had no idea my dog would do such a thing. He laughed and said he was on his way down to get them since it was milking time this time of the day and Lona saved him from walking all that way. He was more than happy. He said he would buy Lona right then and there if I wanted to sell her. He had wished his farm collie would learn to herd but had no luck teaching him. Fowler was as happy as could be that his work was made much easier that day. I was more than just relieved.

On the way home that Sunday, we had a lot to talk about. Lee sat in the front with me and Bruce and Lona in the back. We recounted our experiences and lived them all over again. It didn't take long for Bruce and Lona to fall asleep together in the back seat. It was a beautiful picture of two innocent souls exhausted from the weekend activities, a scene embedded strongly in my mind forever.

A few months later, Lona's herding instinct went into play again. We were walking up the dirt road toward the next farm. When we reached Meyer's property we started to pass a smaller barn when Lona went under the fence into the building. I was puzzled. Why did she do this? Suddenly, a large Ram came running out with Lona right behind. She undoubtedly smelt him inside, went in to investigate, and drove him out into his small fenced in enclosure where she thought he should be. He was bigger than Lona but she was the boss. He did exactly what she wanted him to do. When I called her name she ran over, I put her on the lead and hoped no one at Meyers saw what happened. We headed back fast.

The Chow is not a man developed breed, but one of the original breeds developed by Mother Nature from the wolf. Their DNA is the closest to the wolf of all breeds. They originated in northern China and were used by man for all purposes. There are vases in the Han dynasty almost 2000 years old showing engravings of dogs that look exactly like Chows, and literature referring to the black tongued dog. Somewhere in Lona's inherited background the instinct to herd was still dominate when the occasion to do so presented itself. Their blue black tongue is shared with the polar bear. Did they develop out of a common ancestor? It is a mystery. There is so much we don't know and Mother Nature keeps her secrets very well.

The years flew by. I now lived in Getzville and had a small kennel. We all grew older, and when Lona was five years old I decided to breed her again - this time to a beautiful young show dog I bought from the West Coast Chi-Yan. I showed him and he finished his championship fast. He would be the perfect father to puppies out of Lona. She spent most of her time in the house with Mother during the day while I was at work. In the evening, I would walk Chi-Yan on the lead with Lona running free back through my woods in the rear of my four acres, over a man made bridge and into the huge vacant YMCA camp for a couple of miles to explore each day. It was a rural life and we loved it.

I was very pleased when I found out Lona was pregnant. However, when the sonogram showed only one puppy, the veterinarian felt the one pup would be too large to whelp naturally, and he strongly advised a Caesarean.

The day came for the operation. Lona had been very healthy all nine weeks during the gestation period, ate well and had plenty of exercise each day. I warned the vet that Chows did not take anesthesia very well and breeders had lost more than one when given too much.

I will never forget that day. The vet left the operating room, came into the waiting room for Lona, took the lead and walked her down the hall. All the time Lona kept looking back at me trying to pullback from the vet, and wanting so much to be with me. I was scared and hoped I would not start to cry...I felt a shiver down go my back. I told myself she was in good hands, that all will be fine.

I don't know how long I waited but it seemed forever. When the door to the operating room opened I stood up with a smile on my face. "Is everything o.k.?" Was I hearing right? "I am very sorry Mr. Drennan. We did everything we possibly could. But we lost Lona. I am so sorry."

I couldn't believe what I heard. I screamed "No. No. No." and the tears came streaming out of my eyes. I was in a state of shock.

A dog is as precious to most of us as any human can be. Lona was so close to me....alwys by my side. And now she was dead! How could fate be so cruel?

I don't know how I got home that day with Lona in the back in a plastic bag. The sonogram had shown a female pup. Did the vet give this very healthy dog too much anesthesia? There was no other explanation.

Mother could not believe Lona was dead. She was still crying when I left with Lona to bury her in my woods just off the beaten path where we walked each day.

The soil was soft and rich and the plot was easy to dig deep and wide. When I placed her in the ground I covered it with pine needles. The tears never stopped. I marked the grave with a large white rock....another one of nature's beautiful treasures.

Each day when I walked past her grave, I would remember all the happiness Lona brought into my life. She was only five years old, was gone much, much too soon, but her memory will always live with me. I have had so many wonderful dogs, more than most people ever will. But none shared so many memories with me and other members of the family like Lona did. This made such a difference in choosing my favorite dog of all time.....being able to share so many of those memories with those I love. Lona will never be forgotten.

My Favorite dog - Lona

Mrs. Winston

Back in the early 1960's, I bought a beautiful nine month old male Chow Chow from a kennel on the West Coast, showed him to his championship with top wins and decided to "special" him aiming for Group and Best-In-Show achievements. Chi-Yan was a dark red, heavy boned and with personality plus. It was at the Cleveland, Ohio show that Mrs. Winston came into my life.

Chi-Yan was on the grooming table when a large black woman in her forties approached me with a big smile on her face and many compliments about my beautiful dog. She was very over dressed for a dog show, and sparkled with so many diamonds that there was no doubt in my mind she must be very wealthy. She introduced herself as Mrs. Winston, showed and bred Chow Chows and had lost a champion male a few years ago that reminded her so much of my dog. She said she was so grief stricken when Tyrone died that she could not part with him, and had his body made into a bear-type rug so he would always be with her resting in front of the fire place. Needless to say, I was a little turned off.

Ch. Chi- Yan Kid
Sire of 23 Champions including a multiple Best-In-Show son.

She wanted to know all about my dog, and when I told her Chi-Yan was the son of the well known Ch. Ghat de la Moulaine on the West Coast she grew very excited. Chi-Yan was a natural kisser. I would ask him to give me a kiss on the right cheek and then on the other and he always complied. He learned to do that on my command with strangers and was a big hit.

I asked Mrs. Winston if she would like a kiss from Chi-Yan and she eagerly answer yes. She bent her head over toward Chi-Yan, I gave him the command to give her a kiss. Without hesitating, his blue-black tongue did the job. She squealed with laughter. I then gave Chi-Yan the command to give Mrs. Winston a kiss on the other cheek. Chi-Yan obeyed and Mrs. Winston's laughter was loud and clear. She informed me she had a daughter of Tyrone's she wanted to breed, and now she finally found the stud for Marylin she had been looking for, and that stud was Chi-Yan.

We talked about pedigrees, stud fees, our show wins, judges, etc. and both huge fans of the breed. She informed me Marilyn was due in season soon and she would call me each week to keep me informed.

That Monday I called a friend of mine in Ohio, Mrs. Florence Stanton, a well known Chow exhibitor, to find out if she knew Mrs. Winston. I will never forget the shock I felt when Mrs. Stanton informed me Mrs. Winston's husband was the leader of the black underground criminal activity in the city of Cleveland. He had been in and out of prison many times, once had been charged with murder but was able to beat that rap. I asked if that big black man standing near Mrs. W. at the dog show was her husband. No..that was her bodyguard!

At that point I didn't want to have anything to do with Mrs. W. and moaned....."How do I get out of this?" She said whatever you do don't back out." Your life could be in danger if you did so. Mrs. Winston has never been involved in any criminal activity, all dogs are in her name. You are dealing with her and not him."

So reluctantly, I waited to see if Mrs. W. would call me each week. The answer was yes. She did call each week, was very friendly, her dogs were her life and they had the same care you would give a beloved child. She asked about motels in the area, names and telephone numbers and how far were they from my kennel. Each time she called I wondered if the FBI was listening in. I wished I could get out of this but felt helpless. Mrs. W. asked if Marilyn had pups, would I go down and help her pick out the best pup. I almost bit my tongue but said yes I would.

So three weeks flew by when I got a surprise telephone call from Mrs. Stanton. She said she had good news and bad news for me. The good news was I would not have to breed Chi-Yan to Marilyn after all. I was very surprised and very curious why. Then the bad news. In the morning paper on the front page, Mrs. Winston was found dead on her bed the day before. I was shocked. "What happened? Did her husband kill her." No...that was not the answer. She suffered years from a heart condition, and she died from a severe heart attack.

I felt relieved in one sense of the word yet in the same way I felt sorrow for the loss of my telephone friend, a dog lover with so much in common with me, but really so far apart.

I often wondered what would have happened if her dog had pups, if I had visited her home, and saw what it was like in that other world. It was an adventure never to happen....probably for the best. I felt sad that our breed had lost someone with so much devotion and love for Chows. Her dogs wound their way around her heart the same way mine had done with me. We responded the same way to our precious dogs. Mrs. Winston left this world of Chows much, much too soon.

An Unforgettable Chow

I have found the Chow to be one of the most intelligent dogs, and through the years the breed has proven this to me on more than one occasion. But the one experience that stands out in my mind the most is the story of Dinah, a beautiful red Chow which was sent to me from California three days in season, to be bred to one of my Champion males.

She arrived at the Buffalo, NY airport on a Wednesday evening in early April, and that week it had rained hard every day-breaking all records for the amount of precipitation received in a seven-day period. My kennels are located in the country, and I had moved to this location in December. The kennels and kennel runs were finished on time, but the fence company did not have time to enclose the yard around. the kennels because of our very long winter.

Dinah was put in a kennel on the east side, and I reinforced the gate in the kennel run by driving several very long steel stakes into the ground so she could not dig out. She would not eat her food, so I left it in the kennel hoping she would do so during the night.

In the morning, I found the food had not been touched, and when I looked out the window of the kennel I got the shock of my life. Evidently, she had been digging all night and the hole in the front of the gate was so large and deep that the steel stakes simply fell over and Dinah was gone! I could hardly believe what she had done, but the soft ground from all the rain we had was a big help in Dinah's escape. Here was a dog three days in season, shipped all the way from California, and now among the missing.

I was frantic and immediately notified the S.P.C.A. and the police to be on the look out for a lion-like red Chow, and in my imagination I could see her lying beside the road, a victim of a hit-and-run driver. I notified the farmers in my area, but no one had seen her and I spent the day driving up and down every street, stopping at homes with a picture of a Chow and offering a generous reward for her return.

On Friday, I also stayed home from work and spent the day looking for her. We even tried trained hunting dogs in the hope that they would be able to track her down but I had no luck whatsoever. I rented a large animal trap and placed it in my woods along the path, with meat as a bait, and contacted the owner of a Blood-hound, but found out they use them for humans only and never for other dogs.

Saturday morning arrived and there still was no trace of Dinah. No one had seen her and I felt for sure that I would never get her back. My ad appeared in Friday's evening paper and I spent Saturday morning at home, hoping I might get a *call* giving me at least a clue to where she might have been seen. I had hardly slept for two nights worrying about what might have happened to her.

At exactly 12 PM the phone rang, and a man it the other end of the line asked if I was the man who placed the ad in the paper for the lost Chow. He went on to explain that he was the owner of a private air field about five miles from my home and a dog that looked like a lion had been there for 2½ days, lying along the runway and checking all the airplanes as they came in or out. He said the dog didn't seem to be afraid of the planes at all and went over to everyone as they boarded or arrived. He thought she must belong to one of the neighboring farmers, and had no idea what she had done at night when the airport was closed.

My mind was racing and I explained that she had arrived from California on Wednesday evening, had dug out and was missing until now. Both of us had the same thought-she was looking for a ride back or possibly her master who had left her at the airport three days ago! The connection with the airplanes in her mind meant one thing (call it instinct if you want), a way to get home or to find her master, whom she loved very much.

I rushed to the, airport to get her, and when I arrived the entire crew had surrounded Dinah, but she gave no fight whatsoever when they tied a rope around her neck for a lead. She evidently had been drinking water from the puddles in the runway, and to my surprise was almost as clean as the day she arrived. She made no fuss whatsoever when I placed her in the car, paid my reward and thanked the owner of the airport for all he had done.

Back at the kennel she ate all her food and lay down quietly for a nap. It was almost like a miracle, because in minutes it started to pour and rained especially hard the rest of the day.

Dinah adjusted beautifully for the next two weeks, she was bred to an outstanding Champion male and when it was time to ship her back I hated to see her go. She had grown to be a very special dog for me and one I will never forget. I wish I could say she had a litter of puppies, but for Dinah motherhood would be something she would not experience. However, her love and devotion to her master and outstanding, keen intellectual capacity showed us the most intelligent Chow we had ever known.

Dogs Are The Best Medicine

At one point in the most busy part of my doggy life, I found myself with a three month old male Chow with a very high potential to be a top winner in the show ring. I wanted to place him with the right owner who would train, show and love him the way such a beautiful dog deserved. And lo and behold, the phone rang one Saturday and my wish was about to come true.

The lady on the end of the phone was looking for a Chow puppy her daughter could show. It could act as medicine to help her daughter get over the break up with her fiance just days before the wedding. She was devastated and had become depressed to the point she had to take a leave of absence from her job. Her mother felt the dog would give Pat something to take her mind off her troubles, and bring new happiness into her life.

When I told her about Blaze she felt he was the answer. They arrived at my kennel a few days later. Her daughter, Pat, looked so sad and tired when I met her. That mood didn't last long when she saw Blaze. She knelt to greet him and to my delight, his tail never stopped wagging as he gave her a big kiss on her cheek. Pat smiled and hugged Blaze, and I knew this was a match in heaven. Pat blossomed before my very eyes, a beautiful young woman now with a partner that would love her for life.

As the weeks went by, Pat took Blaze to obedience school to learn the tricks of the trade in the show ring. They both learned fast and were perfect for one another. Pat went back to work and her depression disappeared. Her life revolved around her new companion. He made living worthwhile.

Even better was their first show. It was in another part of the state and unfortunately, I did not have a dog entered. When the phone rang Pat sounded like a gal who had won a million dollars. Blaze earned two points on Saturday and two more on Sunday. I was told later they looked perfect in the ring, and I knew

Blaze would not disappoint her along the way to his championship. At one show, the judge gave Blaze, a class dog, the breed over a champion male shown by one of the top handlers in the country. This does not happen very often and it was a win Pat never forgot. Blaze finished his championship undefeated, which is remarkable in the dog world. It was a fairy tale in more ways than one. It completely changed Pat's look out on life. She gave Blaze all the credit. She was healed.

A year later, she met a gentlemen who later became her husband. He loved dogs too. Dogs bring people together far more often than we ever realize.

I'm Lost. Where is my Mommy?

She Got Even

In the dog world, we meet many people who pass through your life for a short period of time but, for one reason or another, you never forget. Mary MacEashern was one of those people.

She was a competitor at a dog show where I was showing. She introduced herself and I recognized her name from reading about her kennel in dog magazines. I recalled her reputation as an outgoing, happy-go-lucky person she attributed to her winning Chows. She lost that day to my dog, and much to my surprise asked if she could breed a bitch in the near future to him. I was flattered to think my dog impressed this woman, who had been breeding and showing Chows for over 30 years. She would let me know when her dog came in season and ready to breed. That day arrived and I was very pleased to find her black coated dog was one of my liking. There was a 20 minute tie and I predicted her dog conceived and would have pups. Nine week later she had a healthy litter of four. Mary planned to keep the best female. Her dogs made life worth living. She worked as a secretary to a lawyer in a small town in Eastern New York State. However, her husband was the problem. He drank too much, worked too seldom and she hated it when he insisted going to the shows with her....always drinking too much and embarrassing her by telling dirty stories to the women exhibitors. Some complained and suggested ways she could arrange to leave him home. She tried but was not always successful. She claimed at times she would like to cut him up in bits and pieces.

Quite often I would receive calls for puppies. I had about one litter a year so most of the time I had nothing to sell. A young woman with a soft southern accent called looking for a Chow puppy a few weeks after Mary's litter was born. I gave her Mary's telephone number. A few days later, Joanne called to thank me. She bought the one puppy left in the litter, a black female she called Jill. Mary told her the puppy had a heart murmur and did not advise any heavy exercise routines. She was the perfect pet, however, not shy, outgoing and a fast learner. Joanne was estatic.

Mary confided in Joanne that Jill was not show quality, but Joanne wanted to show her at least one time. She brought her to a show when seven months old and much to my surprise, I could not believe what the dog had learned. Chows do not as a rule sit on their rear legs and beg. But Jill did when Joanne awarded her with a tasty dog treat. And Chows don't walk on their hind legs like a poodle in a circus. It was hard for me to believe Jill could do that also.

The next month, a dog show in our area caught Joanne's eye. She informed us she was going to enter. Mary put on her thinking cap and decided to get other Chow exhibitors to enter also, and built up the show for a major in Chows. For a major at that time, you needed six bitches for three points. Believe me, they are hard to find.

Mary had a seasoned older bitch which needed a major to finish her championship. She was pleased that Jill was entered. Without this dog there would not be enough for a three pointer.

Joanne called a couple weeks before the show. She was nervous and wanted to know if I could give her a few pointers on showing her dog. Joanne was a very pretty, sweet young woman in her early twenties, and with her southern accent came across as very charming. I decided I would have some fun at this show. The judge was an older, grey haired man with the reputation of putting up the best looking girl in the ring regardless of what the dog looked like. I suggested to Joanne that a mini skirt would help her to win under this gentlemen. I also suggested when the dogs first enter the ring instead of standing in line like statues, she should have Jill sit up and beg for food. It would impress the judge. I also suggested when the judge had them move around the ring to check their gait, that she start off moving Jill for several feet walking on her back legs only.

You guessed it. Joanne did everything I suggested. The judge was really impressed. I heard him say, "I can't believe a Chow can do these things." He pointed to Joanne, "Winners Bitch." Joanne was smart enough to have Jill walk toward the judge on her hind legs when they walked over to pick up the ribbon. I can still hear her say in her southern accent, "Did I do all right, Mr. Judge?" They stood talking and laughing for a few moments. Joanne left the ring with a big smile on her face and a hug outside the ring for her beloved Jill.

Meanwhile, Mary was a very unhappy gal when her dog went Reserve. She had lost to a dog sold by her as a pet. She started complaining to me - "How did she ever know to dress that way? How did she even know how to show her dog that way? I can't believe it."

It was hard for me to keep from laughing. "I am very surprised too. You have to admit Joanne acted like a professional. She took a chance and came out a winner."

Joanne had promised to never tell Mary I was involved in our little plot to beat her at her own game. She never suspected otherwise. We kept our secret and Joanne was motivated to continue her quest to complete Jill's championship. It worked again and again and a year later Mary was laughing when she called to tell me another dog of her breeding had finished, and that dog was Jill. She praised Joanne for what a good handler she turned out to be

A few months later, Mary called to tell me her husband had died from a heart attack. I extended my sympathy and asked when and where was the wake. She said there wasn't any. She said she hoped that I would not be mad for what she did. I was all ears.

She had finally gotten even with him. Mary often exclaimed how she would like to cut him up in little pieces. She called the University of Rochester medical school and donated his body as a cadaver for medical students to disect piece by piece as part of their learning to be medical doctors. She wanted to know if I thought she did the wrong thing.

I told her it was a very noble thing to do. There was a shortage of cadavers and it would help medical students in so many ways to learn about many parts of the human body. I congratulated her on an excellent decision.

Mary continued to show dogs until she retired in her sixties and moved to California to be with her sister. I have a beautiful silver plated candy dish she donated at a show for Best of Breed. It sits on a table with my tape recorder. Each time I turn it on I see the dish and think of Mary. The soft, relaxing music brings back those happy memories from years ago which I will never forget.

"The Man In The Wheelchair"

My top winning Chow Chow was the No. one Chow in the United States defeating more dogs than any other Chow shown that year. He had been unbeaten in the breed and in this particular weekend, we were heading down to Ohio to show Van Van in the Sugarbush dog show.

For those not familiar with dog shows, a dog must get the breed first, then compete in the Group and win first place before competing with the winners from the other Groups for Best-In-Show. That big win was what my handler, Bud Moser, and I were hoping for.

We arrived at the show in plenty of time to groom Van Van and enable him to get adjusted to the new surroundings when a friend, Mrs. Florence Stanton, approached the table all smiles with compliments about my beautiful dog. She was a member of the

Sugarbush Kennel Club, and informed me there was something I should know. I was all ears.

It seems one of the most active members in their club was dying from cancer, and he had always hoped and prayed that some day his Old English Sheepdog might go Best-In-Show. The Board of Directors got together and decided they were going to make it happen.

They contacted the breed judge, who was also judging the Herding Group, and the Best-In-Show judge and asked them to make their friend's wish come true at this show, and bring much happiness into his life before he died. This is illegal, of course, but they didn't care. Morally, to them it was the right thing to do.

Mrs. Stanton couldn't wait to tell me what was going on....that we would not go Best-In-Show. She felt I would understand. I told her there were other shows in the future where we would have a chance again at the big win, but this man would never have another opportunity to do so.

When I told Bud Moser, he hit the ceiling. He felt it was very dishonest and never should have been planned this way by the club. If it happens at this show, then it must happen at other shows for who knows what reason. Bud felt it was pure politics. He said he was going to make sure Van Van showed better than he ever had and make it obvious which dog should win.

Van Van got the breed and first in the Non-Sporting Group. The Old English got the breed and Group one in the Herding Group. The judge went over all the seven winners and brought out the Chow and the Old English trying to decide which would go Best-In-Show.

Van Van showed like a dream, head up and not a step out of place as this beautiful red flaming coated dog moved around the ring. I liked the Old English, but in no way did he compare to my dog.

When the judge pointed to the Old English for Best-In-Show the shouts and clapping in the room were deafening. I looked at the owner in the wheelchair and the tears of happiness ran down his cheek. It was his dream come true. I felt his happiness and could understand better than ever why his friends had planned it this way.

However, Bud did not agree. He thought all wins should be on the up and up regardless of the situation. But life is very unpredictable and nothing is ever 100% certain.

So there you have it. You take sides. For me, later that year we did again go Best-In-Show. We had another chance and won, but the man in the wheelchair didn't. He died a few weeks later long before his time. Who was the lucky one....him or me?

Did He Really Cheat?

Bud Moser was my dog handler. His biography: He served four years on a Navy ship during the second World War, came home, married his high school sweetheart, had three children, was a blue collar worker at a factory in Buffalo and needed more money to support his family. He loved dogs and was hired as an assistant to a well known professional handler to help him at dog shows most weekends.

When I needed someone to show my champion Chow Chow Bud was highly recommended. I expected to see a tall imposing man since he worked mostly with large breeds. Instead, I was surprised to find him to be 5' 5" tall and weighing about 120 pounds. But he made up in size with his unique ability to move around the ring with grace and style. He was a pleasure to watch. In the show ring, Bud knew how to get the most out of handling a dog.

At this particular time there were no shows within driving distance so I looked forward to a couple of weekends staying home. Bud called me and asked if I would do him a favor. He told his wife that the next weekend he was going down to Youngstown, Ohio to show Don's champion Chow. If she should call, never admit otherwise.

When I asked why, he told me the whole story. One of the men he worked with's hobby was driving to Youngstown on Saturdays to attend a theatre where strippers were allowed to take off all their clothes. He subscribed to "Stripper" magazine and it kept him informed which stripper was the headline each week. That particular Saturday Irma The Body would be there. Bud wanted to see her because the magazine's biography informed him she showed Cardigan Welsh Corgis and recently had finished the championship on a male she was now specialing. I think the dog gave him an excuse to go with his friend, but the real draw was Irma flaunting her naughty self.

I assured him I would keep his secret. He said the Stockton, N.Y. show was scheduled the next month and he hoped to meet Irma and encourge her to enter this show. He promised when he got back, and when his wife was out shopping, he would call me and share his experiences. He was very excited. This was a big deal in his life and a secret he wanted to share with me.

I did get a call from him the next week. He had a most enjoyable time and an experience he would never forget. I now have the opportunity to relate his story to you. It is one that most of us would never have, but one that makes unordinary people like Bud that more interesting.

That particular Saturday the matinee was scheduled for 2:00 P.M. and Bud and his friend arrived an hour and half ahead of time. All ready there was a line of fifteen men ahead of them. Bud's friend carried a flashlight and explained all the lights were not turned on when the doors opened and he needed the flashlight to find their way down to the front row for the best seats. And they were lucky. They got two seats in the front row middle to their great delight.

While they waited for the show to begin, Bud got the idea of sending a note with the usher to Irma backstage. He wrote that he was a professional dog show handler and had come all the way from Buffalo to see her, talk about dog shows and judges and to hear all about her beautiful dogs. Bud gave the usher a tip and he promised to deliver his note backstage to Irma.

The show finally began. The all female chorus danced out first with the usual big fans seemingly hiding what was in the middle. When the fans moved back - you guessed it - there was Irma all in a white revealing negligee. I forgot what followed but Bud enjoyed every minute. Somewhere along the way Irma stopped the show to ask if Bud Moser would raise his hand so she could give him a message. Bud's hand went up fast. Irma announce she had his note referring to her dogs and she was going to do a dance especially for him. Bud felt a little embarrassed but that soon passed when Irma performed an erotic dance in front of him on the stage that caused him to arise to the occasion when the dance ended with Irma completely naked. At that point she invited him after the show to meet her backstage in her dressing room. Bud was thrilled beyond words. His plan had worked.

The show was a big success according to Bud. The usher guided him backstage to Irma's dressing room. She was modestly dressed, gave him a big hug, brought out framed pictures of her dogs and according to Bud they laughed and talked about dogs for the next half hour.

She also told him a few personal things about herself. She started her dancing career when only fifteen years old. She was born with a natural excellent figure and at maturity, her knockers were 38" in the morning and 40" at night. Bud couldn't figure out why they would be two inches larger at night.

She promised to enter the Stockton show, would bring her Special and a class male and asked Bud to assist her at the show ring since she would be alone and needed help. I asked him if she kissed him goodbye when he left. He said she kissed him on the lips and at the same time she kissed him on the lips, she touched him in places where he had never been touched before by anyone else but his wife.

"Bud. You cheated on your wife!" Bud said - "No way. She was the aggresor. She took me by surprise. I guess she thought I was so sexy looking she just couldn't resist."

I had a hard time not laughing....a skinny man in his fifties, weighing 120 pounds - far less than Irma - thinks he is sexy?"

So you be the judge. Did Bud cheat on his wife, or was it just a friendly little bit of affection because they both loved dogs so much? Regardless, it was one of the most enjoyable and unforgettable days in Bud Moser's life.

The Stockton dog show arrived. Bud found Irma at her motor home and he helped her groom her dogs. I was over to the ring waiting for Cardigan Corgis to be judged. The judge was an older overweight man in his seventies. Then Bud arrived under the tent to pick up her arm bands, and behind him Irma arrived with her two dogs. Bud helped her put on the arm bands. I got a good look at Irma, who towered over Bud by several inches. To my surprise, she was very modestly dressed. However, her clothes fit like a glove and showed off her ample figure. She had told Bud she was 28. Believe me, she looked all of 38!

There were two class dogs. The other Corgi was shown by its owner..a much older woman. When Irma moved around the ring with her dog it wasn't hard to tell she was very experienced in making the most of her natural endowments..She knew how to wiggle that rear and the judge (like they show in the movies) could not take his eyes off Irma. She got the one point and thanked the judge with a big smile.

Then it was time to change dogs. She handed the class dog to Bud to handle and took her champion dog in for Best of Breed. The judge practically ignored Bud but took a great deal of time going over Irma's Special. They talked and Irma had him laughing when her dog went Best of Breed. She wanted a picture taken.

At this point Irma held the lead of the class dog in one hand and with the other her champion. However, for some reason or other the dogs would not stand but insisted on lying down on the ground. Irma fixed that. She sat on the ground with one dog on the left and the other on the right lying beside her. The judge stood behind

Irma holding one ribbon with his left hand over the class dog, and the other ribbon held over the Special when the picture was taken. I can never remember seeing a show picture set up where the winners were all sitting on the ground. Irma gave the judge a little pat on the arm and a big smile when they parted.

I understand a couple years later Irma married a much older man and disappeared from the limelight. She was unforgetable.

**Secret Lives**

I met Bert and Bernice Hardy, Berlin Center, Ohio, at a dog show in the Buckeye State and liked them immediately with their down-to-earth happy-go-lucky dispositions. They were a heavy set couple in their seventies, had recently lost their beloved elderly Chow and were very impressed with the dog I was showing. They were in the market for a puppy, and wanted a female like the one they lost. They never had children and dogs were their devoted substitute.

The Hardies were in luck. Lona, my most favorite dog, was expecting pups and I promised I would let them know when the pups were born. I knew from talking to them that a dog would have the best home ever with this sweetheart couple.

They were in luck. Lona had three puppies - all females. I had one sold to a young woman in West

Virginia, decided to keep one, and the third would go to the Hardies in Ohio.

I will never forget how excited Bert was when I called him with the good news. He would drive to Kenmore in about seven weeks to pick her up, and insisted on calling each week for a first hand account on how the pups were progressing. Bert and Bernice both acted like expectant parents looking forward to this wonderful moment in their lives when the puppy would be a loving part of their family.

The day arrived and they arrived on time, on a Saturday morning, to pick up their little girl. I will never forget how they laughed with joy when I brought out the puppy I had reserved for them. They were like two children with a new toy. And to my delight, the puppy wagged her tail sixty miles an hour when she saw them, and each got a kiss on the cheek when they took turns holding her in their arms. It was a perfect day for all of us. They promised to call the next day to report on how she adapted to her new home and to let me know the name they chose for her. They did as they promised.

They loved a comic strip at the time called "Lulu" and that is how Lona's daughter got her name.

Bert would write me about Lulu from time to time and whenever I entered a show in their area I always stopped in to see them and Lulu. They made you feel so much at home, like you had known them all your life. Bernice always baked me an apple pie. My dog handler, Bud, was always with me on each visit and he also would enjoy a piece of pie. What was left, Bernice would wrap up to take home with me. However, Bernice put so much sugar in the pie it tasted like raw sugar, which is the direct opposite from what I enjoy. I had to fib and tell her it was very tasty. The little lie made her happy so I felt I did the right thing.

About the same time, other Ohioians came into my life. This couple had purchased a red male from an associate of mine in Ohio - both the sire and dam from my breeding. They were looking forward to showing him and met me at a show where Bert and Bernice were present. I introduced this seventies couple to Bob and Dorothy Fosnaugh, a much younger couple in their thirties, childless. Their dog also was a substitute for the child they never had. We all had one thing in common, and hit it off very well. Bob was a tool and die maker, tall and good looking, and Dorothy was blonde and very attractive. Friendships were cemented that day.

There were dog shows every weekend in Ohio, which was not true in Western New York. The Ohio shows were a draw for me and from time to time, my new friends would visit with us at one, or in the case of the Hardies, I would stop in to see them and Lulu after the Sunday show on our way home to New York State.

A year or so later, I got a call from Bob Fosnaugh with shocking news. Dorothy had been killed in an auto accident, and Bob wanted to know if I would take his dog temporarily until he got over the shock and got some semblance of normality back in his life. I drove down to get the dog and Bob was beside himself with grief. He had been working so much overtime he knew the dog was being neglected and he wanted only the best care for his pet.

He said the day after the funeral, the doorbell rang and when he opened it a young woman stood there holding the hand of a little girl about four. She said she read about the accident and extended her heartfelt sympathy. Bob thanked her. She then said she was there to take his wife's place, that she could do anything his wife could do. Bob could hardly believe what he was hearing. "If you can do anything my wife could do, then pick up this dog and put it on the grooming table." She was aghast. "You know I can't do that." "Then you get the hell out of here fast and don't ever, ever come near this home again."

He slambed the door, clenched his fists and couldn't believe any woman looking for a free home to live had the nerve to proposition him that way.

Months went by. Bob soon felt lost without his dog so Buster went home to his master. The Hardies kept in touch and I promised to stop in to see them after the show that particular weekend. When Bud and I walked in we were surprised to see Bob Fosnaugh. "Hi Bob. Bert told me you were going to be at the show two weeks ago. I looked for you and you didn't show up. What happened?"

He went on to explain that he was there. "Then why didn't you find me." He asked if I remembered the woman with the big hat standing about fifty feet away - standing looking at me, disappearing and returning from time to time.

"Sure I remember. I wondered why she didn't come over to talk. I thought she must be shy."

"Well that woman in the big hat was me."

Was I hearing right? The woman in the big hat was Bob? "You mean the woman in the hat was you - dressed as a woman?"

"I knew you would be surprised, and was afraid you might resent that I am a cross dresser. I thought it best to disappear instead."

I was speechless for a moment. I told him he was the first cross dressing man I ever knew. Tell me about it I am interested. Why?"

Bob mentioned Dorothy knew all about his cross dressing before he married her. He didn't know the reason himself, but it was something he felt he was born with. He was not a gay man, but got a lot of fun dressing up like a woman. Dorothy used to go with him in public and do all the talking Bob would say nothing. Dorothy was very acceptable, and both had a lot of fun pretending.

A few minutes later Bernice Hardie spoke up. "Don, if you are surprised at this, how about another surprise. That's why Bob and Bert have so much in common. Bert is that way too. He always liked to dress up as a woman like Bob. They both have gone out on a Saturday night together and have a lot of fun."

Was I hearing right? Bert was a cross dresser also! Bernice said she went out with them once, but they had more fun doing it together.

Bob asked if I wanted to see the album of their pictures taken at bars, country fairs, restaurants, etc. Believe me, looking at those pictures no one would ever believe these two men were women. They looked ridiculous to me.....Holloween jokes.

Bob actually had dresses, make up, and wigs at Bert's home just in case on the spur of the moment they might want to go out on the town. Bob asked if we would like to see him dressed as a woman. I explained that was not necessary after seeing them in so many pictures.

Bert was laughing throughout most of this. He said it was all in fun. They did no harm to anyone, got a kick out of it and enjoyed watching the surprised faces of others they met along the way

All this time Bud was speechless. I knew he would have much to say on the ride home. I told our hosts, if Mother Nature planned you this way, no harm is done in this unusual role, then enjoy it. Life is too short to judge anyone on the uncommon aspects of their life.

When we left, Bernice had wrapped up what was left of her apple pie to take home and "enjoy" the next day. We wished everyone good luck, enjoyed our evening and looked forward to seeing them again at another show.

On the way home, Bud and I both wondered why men would want to cross dress and flaunt themselves in public. It was beyond our comprehension. To me, both men were unforgetable. Both found happiness in a most unordinary way. To each his own....Bert and Bob!

My First Bouvier - Fire

I had been very successful breeding and showing Chow Chows for many years Now it was time to devote more time to obedience training. There are three levels in the obedience ring - Novice, Open and Utility. The Novice is similar to the eighth grade level, the Open to a high school graduate and the Utility comparable to a college diploma. I was reaching for the Utility level.

Do you have something to eat for me?

Chows have a very heavy coat, and hot weather is not for them. Most shows are outdoors in the spring, summer and fall, and sitting in the hot sun for upwards of three minutes for the sit and down exercises without moving, is a no no and the physical excertion required by the jumps, is just too hot for the Chow to complete as required. Therefore, I needed another breed where the heat was not a factor. I chose a herding breed, the Bouvier, to fulfill my requirements.

I located a kennel in the Washington, D.C. area, and flew down to pick out my puppy when she was seven weeks old. The breeder picked me up at the airport, and when I saw her adult dogs and the mother to the puppies, I knew I had made the right choice.

There were three females in the litter. The breeder thought the largest one would be right for me. Instead, I choice Fire, the middle one, very outgoing and not afraid of anything. She was the start of a new adventure with me. Little did I know our adventures together would start that day.

The breeder furnished a crate for Fire and drove us back to the airport for our trip home. Fire was checked in as luggage to Buffalo, N. Y. so that went smoothly. However, at the ticket counter I was told that the entire passenger list had been bumped to make room for a very high level of Japanese government executives who had taken over the entire plane. I would have to take a later flight, one which would make my arrival in Buffalo three hours late. My original plane took off with Fire in the baggage department. She would arrive three hours ahead of me. I called Bud, my handler, and asked him to pick her up at the Buffalo airport, and if everything else went as scheduled, I would be at his home about 1:00 A.M. in the morning.

Later, I found out Bud arrived in plenty of time to rescue Fire. However, they told him she was on the plane, but scheduled to go on to Toronto, the final meeting place for the Japanese. After a long discussion with the airport aurhorities, they admitted their mistake and released Fire to Bud. I picked her up at Bud's home at 1:00 A.M. as scheduled. They had been having a great time playing with Fire, and Bud's wife had fallen in love with her sunny, sweet disposition and congratulated me on choosing such a real charmer. I thought to myself - "What a start this is. Whoever would dream I would have such an unusual experience on my first day of ownership with Fire. If this is any example what will happen in the future, there will never be a dull moment in the months to come."

I didn't have to worry. From that time on, Fire was a joy and pleasure to work with. I entered her in an obedience class taught by a Dutchman, who had been trained by experts in Europe. At six months of age, I started to show Fire at shows in both conformation and obedience at the same time. She was all I had hoped for and finished her requirements for the Novice obedience title and American Kennel Club championship title at only fifteen months old.

At home, she was the perfect companion who kept me amused and delighted with her unique personality. The Bouvier always greets you with a wagging tail plus a bow with their front legs. The bowing comes easy and I enjoyed watching her go through this routine several times a day. Fire had a little soft elf like toy she carried around with her in the house. It was this toy that gave me the idea to teach her how to play hide-and-go-seek. From my living room, the long hallway toward the front of the house is the route to three bedrooms and two baths. I started by putting Fire on the long down in the living room, then walking down the hall to a bedroom. In the bedroom I would place the toy for her to find....always within physical reach. I would give her the command to "go fetch." She would bound into the bedroom I had just left to find the toy. Then you never saw such a happy dog return to the living room with her find. She was so excited! The look on her face was precious. She found the toy and drank in the praise I bestowed on her. This was the event of the day. Her happiness was contagious

I found I had to go in all three bedrooms and baths with the toy. If I entered only one, my scent was a giveaway. When my scent was in all rooms, it made it harder for her to find the toy.

Fire also completed her Open obedience title. Time flew by and she was almost two years old, and it was time for her to become a mother. Her breeder had moved to California, had imported an outstanding male from France, and he was now an American champion. He would be perfect to father a litter out of Fire. I shipped her to California a few days before she would be ready to breed. She arrived in good condition, adjusted to her new surrounding was bred twice and returned to me. Breeders of all breeds have often found their bitches, for some reason or another, often do not conceive when long trips like this are made. This was not a problem with Fire. She definitely was in whelp. She got plenty of exercise, the best food and care and the nine week gestation period arrived before I knew it.

As I sat eating my evening meal, Fire was resting in the corner of the kitchen in her favorite spot. Dogs shed most of their belly fur so the bare skin made it easy to watch the kicking of the puppies in her abdomen. At times it was so uncomfortable she would get up and move. Along about 10:00 P.M. I put her on the lead for an outing in her kennel run before going to bed. At this point, I noticed a contraction and knew labor had started. She relieved herself in the run, and by the time I got her in the whelping box a puppy popped out. I could hardly believe my eyes how fast her first puppy came into the world. I removed the sack, cut the cord, (Fire ate the afterbirth.) shook the pup down to make sure there was no water in the passageways, dried him off with a warm towel and placed him beside Fire to mother. She knew exactly what to do, gave him a good bath with her tongue and laid down to let him nurse. What a beautiful picture....Mother Nature's miracle come to life.

A few minutes later, Fire stood up to deliver puppy N. 2. It was another male and he arrived almost as fast as number one. The first pup was put in a nearby carton on a heating pad covered with a bath towel to keep him warm. His stomach was full and he was very content. Within two hours, Fire had whelped seven healthy puppies - five males and two bitches. I was thrilled. It amazed me to watch Fire with her inborn instinct to accomplish all she did and remain calm and collected. Pregnancy and birth are very similar in dogs as it in humans. No wonder scientists worldwide like to use dogs (if possible) as their main choice for research.

Incidentally, the placenta (afterbirth) is eaten by the mother in the animal world to furnish her with food and nutrients. It contains hormones which aid normal labor and stimulates milk production. Recently, in the human world, many obstetricians are recommending parts of the placenta be cooked and fed to mothers with the same benefits as those in animals. Mother Nature knows best.

The puppies grew like little weeds. Fire was a fantastic mother and had loads of milk. To watch them grow each day, eyes opening, standng and walking and eventually playing with one another, was a joy you never forget. Puppies are so much fun.

I didn't have to introduce the pups to puppy food until they were four weeks old. Fire allowed them to nurse off and on till about the sixth week when those sharp little puppy teeth started to hurt her when they nursed. They would approach her to nurse. She then actually would pick them up and "throw" them away from her. They were never hurt but would let out a yelp and hide under a chair or in a corner. It was unusual for a dog to do this, but so funny to watch. The pups were weaned fast.

At seven weeks they were placed in kennel runs - three in one and four in the other. I would let all seven out in the big yard and they would play and romp for long periods of time enjoying the exercise until they would fall asleep just like human babies.

One day I opened the gate to the large outside grassy area surrounding my home. They followed me wherever I wandered. At the same time, they could have gone off by themselves, but it never happened. They reminded me of the mother duck and her ducklings following in such perfect order. It was obvious. I was the pups' master and at no time were they going to let me get out of their sight.

At nine weeks, three of the male puppies left for their new homes. I kept the two bitches and two of the males. Gaby became an American Kennel Club champion. Hero earned his Novice and Open titles in the USA, and all titles, including Utility, in Canada. Honey earned all her obedience titles to Utility in both the U.S. and Canada. Hunter earned all three titles both in the U.S. and Canada and became a television star.

With so many titles, Fire's offspring automatically made her a Register of Merit bitch by the AKC, a most prestigious and difficult award to earn. She lived in excellent health to the ripe old age of fifteen years and three months. She had everything you wanted in a dog, health, personality, brains and companionship. Her image is imprinted in my mind today as strong as ever. How could I have been so lucky to have owned and loved such a wonderful dog?

Unforgettable—Honey

My association with dogs has been so close for so many years that any "family" memory would be incomplete without one story about my beloved animals. There are so many I could write about it would fill a book, but the one that will always be extra vivid in my mind is about Honey, a Bouvier des Flandre,

Honey was born on August 12, 1983, in a litter of five males and two bitches. She wasn't the outstanding pup in the litter by any means, made no special impression as a young puppy, but as a breeder it was very important for me to keep the two bitches for future breeding plans.

Being the smallest, Honey was always picked on by her larger brothers and sister. She didn't hesitate to participate in their rough and tumble games, but was the first to make herself scarce when the games became too rough.

I'm sad. Where is My Master

Honey had the most beautiful, soft brown eyes full of love and adoration. She was very sensitive to my moods and when things would go wrong she sensed it immediately. She would always put her head on my lap in doggy sympathy. She was well named...as sweet as honey.

She was funny too. As a young pup, she loved to put her paws in her drinking dish and splash the water all over. Once, when my back was turned, she picked her dish up off the kitchen counter—filled with dry food—without spilling a single piece. And she loved to shake hands. When she learned to sit on command I started to spell the word S-I-T. And she sat. I did the same with the "drop" command. She would respond immediately both ways...whether by voice or by spelling the words. Her audience loved it.

As she grew older, it was obvious she wasn't afraid of anything. I could let her off lead on our walks through the woods each day and she would always stay close by. Twice, when she approached trespassers she stood her ground directly in front of the startled men barking and growling threatening. They froze in their footsteps. This type of spirit—not afraid of anything— is important in an obedience dog.

I started her training early and she was a fast learner She attended class each week and I trained her five or six times a week in my side yard. There were two medium size ash trees growing just eight feet apart, which were ideal for training her on lead for the figure eight. This exercise required her to walk briskly twice completely around and between the two trees (two stewards are used in the show ring) and on command from the judge, to forward and halt at his discretion. This was a favorite spot for us to stand and start each exercise.

For those who don't know, there are three different titles a dog can earn in obedience, A dog must qualify under three different judges with a score of 170 or better out of 200 in order to earn its title. The Companion title is equivalent to the eighth grade level, the Companion Excellent title to high school, and the most difficult—the Utility title—to a college diploma.

Honey earned her C.D. and C.D.X. in the United States and Canada with few problems, always placing high in each division. Very few dogs ever earn the Utility title. There are at least 250 ways a dog can fail in this class.

Let me briefly explain what a dog must accomplish in order to earn this title. The dog is off lead. The healing exercise requires hand signals only to sit, drop, come and leave the dog on command. In the scent discrimination exercise, ten small dumbbells are used...five made from wood and five from leather. The handler puts his scent on two articles—one wood and one leather. The dog must bring back the right one (all are numbered) or the dog fails the exercise. (In Canada, three sets are used—wood, leather and metal.)

Three gloves are used in the directed retrieve exercise. The gloves are placed at the back of the ring...one in the middle and one at each corner. The dog and handler have their back to the judge. The handler never knows which glove the judge will have the dog retrieve on command.

The directed jumping requires a high jump placed on one side of the ring, and a bar jump on the other side. The dog must go straight back to the other end of the ring and sit on command. Then at the direction of the judge, it must either jump over the high or the bar jump. This is repeated twice so each jump is used. Honey had to jump three feet.

The stand for examination required 12 dogs to stand close to each other in the middle of the ring. The judge examines each dog and the dog must not move. He does this for all 12 dogs and no movement of the feet is allowed.

Honey earned one leg in Utility in the States and two in Canada. I then decided to fly her to Chicago to a specialty show for Bouviers only. This show drew dogs from all over the United States and was one of the most prestigious shows held for this breed. It was a big thrill for me when Honey placed first in Utility with a score of 193 out of 200...the only dog to qualify in this most difficult class.

Next was the third and final show in Canada for leg No. 3. There were 19 dogs in the Utility class...very large for any show, and Honey was once again first in her class with a score of 193. A Bouvier breeder congratulated me on her win, and had recently lost a dog to cancer. She examined Honey and much to my dismay, she found two swollen glands in her neck and suggested I have her tested immediately by my vet. The next day he did a biopsy and I Was shocked to learn that Honey had lymphosarcoma...a very fast moving cancer. He predicted she would be dead in three months if I didn't put her on chemo and special cancer fighting pills. This I did immediately.

I was in a state of shock. Honey had just earned her Utility title in Canada. She needed one more leg in the States and was dying from cancer. The pills and chemo made her very sick for two or three days each week. This program would last seven weeks and the vet informed me she would lose her coat. In addition, she would have to urinate often. It was part of the after effects of the chemo. She was only three years old.

I had her entered at two shows just three weeks from her diagnosis. It would give me a chance to try for that last leg before she dropped all her coat. Honey became very quiet and lethargic. She didn't feel well and yet tried to please me on the days when we were able to train. Her beautiful brown eyes looked so sad.

The Saturday of the first show finally arrived. Both shows were for obedience dogs only. I wrote the column each month for the national obedience paper FRONT & FINISH, covering the news in the North-Eastern part of the United States so I knew most of the people showing at these trials. News soon spread about Honey and her quest to earn that last leg. At this trial she did very well until the stand for examination. She had to urinate, fouled the ring, and was disqualified.

She had one more chance on Sunday. I withheld all water in the morning. She often had the urge to go and would squat often. It was time to enter the ring. Dozens of exhibitors wished me luck, and the ring was surrounded by people watching and hoping Honey would qualify.

Needless to say, I was a nervous wreck. I reached down and petted Honey on the head, removed her lead and walked into the ring. It is so easy for a handler to make an error and cause the dog not to qualify. I tried to concentrate on every exercise and keep calm. This was our last chance and all those people were watching. The only sound at the show was the voice of the judge.

I knew Honey wanted to please me as she had done so many times before. I really don't remember how I got through each exercise. Somehow I did, but I remember vividly the clapping and shouting as Honey finished without any major errors, and earned that last leg in Utility.

I'll always remember that day, my tears of sadness and happiness, but especially the kindness of so many people. A dog's love is unconditional, and dogs bond people close together in fellowship. We all love our dogs and identify with each other...especially when tragedy strikes. It could happen to anyone.

Weeks later Honey took a turn for the worst. Her time on earth was short, She was lying on the floor in the kitchen—her favorite spot in the corner—when she left me. I was so lucky to have owned and trained this very special, lovable dog. She had brought so much happiness into my life.

I buried her under the two ash trees where we stood so many times during our training time together. One tree had started to die. However, the next spring it was once more covered with leaves. Each time I walk there and look at that tree, I wonder if Honey was the reason it now is so healthy and beautiful. She will never be forgotten.

Happiness

When I look back on my life I realize it is not always the big things in life that bring you the most happiness. There are so many lesser events, many that are repeated often, routines you look forward to each day that bring that warm feeling of contentment and joy.

I am fortunate to live on a ten acre spread surrounded by hundreds of pine and deciduous trees. The large open lawn on one side of my home was ideal for setting up the jumps and obedience equipment to train my Bouviers for their Utility titles. There is just enough shade in this wide open area to make it a most comfortable place to train my dogs.

Where we obedience train each day with
that forest face always watching

It is quiet and peaceful and the sky above is breathtaking with its amazing blue color and snowy white clouds floating quietly by. The air has a faint scent of pine and occasionally a bird is seen in the trees, perhaps wondering what we are doing there. It is sharing my time with Mother Nature in all her glory. I stand looking upward at the sky listening to the faint rustle of the leaves in the breeze, and so thankful I have this heavenly spot to enjoy with my beloved dogs.

With no distractions, the dogs venture through their routines beyond my expectations. If only they would do the same in the dog shows! This training ground made training a pleasure, never captured elsewhere, a feeling of happiness.

In this open space, all the ashes from my beloved dogs are spread. On the perimeter of the area, some are actually buried. In the spring, summer and fall, the grass always stays an extra bright green. I ask myself, is this because my dog's ashes are so loved by Mother Nature they have a magical touch, and make this sacred spot more beautiful than it ever would be otherwise? I also want my ashes spread here to join the dogs who brought more memories and happiness into my life than I ever dreamed possible. We all go back to dust from whence we came. I trust others will find the same happiness I have found in this most unusual way.

My First Bouvier, Fire, ready to go to work.

Ch. Van Van. with handler
Multiple Best-In-Show winner, including a
Group Three and then a Group One at the
most prestigious Westmister Dog Show.

Just Back from vacation.

I feel grumpy today

Now I am almost home.

Looking out the window for my master

Good Bye and Good Luck!

About the Author

Don Drennan is a retired steel company administrator whose passion has always been his love for dogs. As a young man, he established as a hobby the Dre-Don Kennels and has bred and shown many dogs to become champions. He also has trained and shown three dogs to their obedience utility titles. He is a charter member of the Kennel Club of Niagara Falls and a past president.

In 1987–1990, Don wrote, directed, and produced for Jones and Adelphia Cable TV, the weekly You and Your Dog series shown in the western New York area. It was one of the first animal shows on cable, and it featured dog owners and their dogs from the immediate vicinity.

In this book, he shares with you stories of the many people from all walks of life who came into his life because of their love for dogs. Don's favorite quote comes from an unknown author: "Dogs are our children who never grow up."

Printed in the United States
By Bookmasters